FOUR SEASONS POETRY BOOKS

WINTER

COMPILED BY JENNIFER WILSON

ILLUSTRATED BY GRAHAM COOPER

Macdonald

Contents

Prelude I   *by T.S. Eliot*   4
Fox   *by Laurence Smith*   5
The Horseman   *by Walter de la Mare*   6
Windy Nights   *by Robert Louis Stevenson*   7
A Fox Came into My Garden   *by Charles Causley*   8
Little Trotty Wagtail   *by John Clare*   9
Winter   *by William Shakespeare*   10
The Sniffle   *by Ogden Nash*   11
Snow in the Suburbs   *by Thomas Hardy*   12
Sparrow   *by Norman MacCaig*   13
Winter Poem   *by Gerda Mayer*   14
Santa Claus   *by Clive Sansom*   15
What the Donkey Saw   *by U.A. Fanthorpe*   16
A Peculiar Christmas   *by Roy Fuller*   17
Halfway Down   *by A.A. Milne*   18
The Black Cloud   *by W.H. Davies*   19
Snowball Wind   *by Aileen Fisher*   20
Dust of Snow   *by Robert Frost*   21
In December   *by Charles Tomlinson*   22
Questioning Faces   *by Robert Frost*   23
Small, Smaller   *by Russell Hoban*   24
End of a Cold Night   *by Norman MacCaig*   25
The Old Wife and the Ghost   *by James Reeves*   26
At Middle-Field Gate in February   *by Thomas Hardy*   28
A Patch of Old Snow   *by Robert Frost*   29
Death of a Snowman   *by Vernon Scannell*   30
Last Snow   *by Andrew Young*   31

Introduction

'To make' is a hard-working verb. We can make friends and models, a garden or fire and sometimes a mess! Making is not easy because when you put many things together to make something new so many things can go wrong.

Each person who makes something also does it in his or her special way. For example, we can follow every detail of a recipe but the cake we have made may not look much like the mouth-watering picture in the cookery book. We have used the right ingredients but put them together in a slightly different way. Poets use words as the ingredients to make a verse. If they are skilful with words they can make us see things in a new way. We all use words every day to say what we feel, but a poet is like a master chef who creates something new and special out of the ingredients.

You will have your own ideas about winter and I wonder how well they will match the wintery thoughts of the poets in this book.

Jennifer Wilson

Prelude I

The winter evening settles down
With smells of steaks in passageways.
Six o'clock.
The burnt-out ends of smoky days.
And now a gusty shower wraps
The grimy scraps
Of withered leaves about your feet
And newspapers from vacant lots;
The showers beat
On broken blinds and chimney-pots,
And at the corner of the street
A lonely cab-horse steams and stamps.
And then the lighting of the lamps.

T.S. Eliot
from Preludes

Fox

Sun plushed eve
and mauve the chilly air
Ice brittle grass squeaks
and creaks as the lone
fox
trips his slinky way
along the inky hedge
He barks and splits the misty air with his
gasping yell.

Laurence Smith

The Horseman

I heard a horseman
    Ride over the hill;
The moon shone clear,
    The night was still;
His helm was silver,
    And pale was he;
And the horse he rode
    Was of ivory.

Walter de la Mare

Windy Nights

Whenever the moon and stars are set,
    Whenever the wind is high,
All night long in the dark and wet,
    A man goes riding by.
Late in the night when the fires are out,
Why does he gallop and gallop about?

Whenever the trees are crying aloud,
    And ships are tossed at sea,
By, on the highway, low and loud,
    By at the gallop goes he.
By at the gallop he goes, and then
By he comes back at the gallop again.

Robert Louis Stevenson

A Fox Came into My Garden

A fox came into my garden.
'What do you want from me?'
'Heigh-ho, Johnnie-boy,
A chicken for my tea.'

'Oh no, you beggar, and never, you thief,
My chicken you must leave,
That she may run and she may fly
From now to Christmas Eve.'

'What are you eating, Johnnie-boy,
Between two slices of bread?'
'I'm eating a piece of chicken-breast
And it's honey-sweet,' I said.

'Heigh-ho, you diddling man,
I thought that was what I could smell.
What, some for you and none for me?
Give us a piece as well!'

Charles Causley

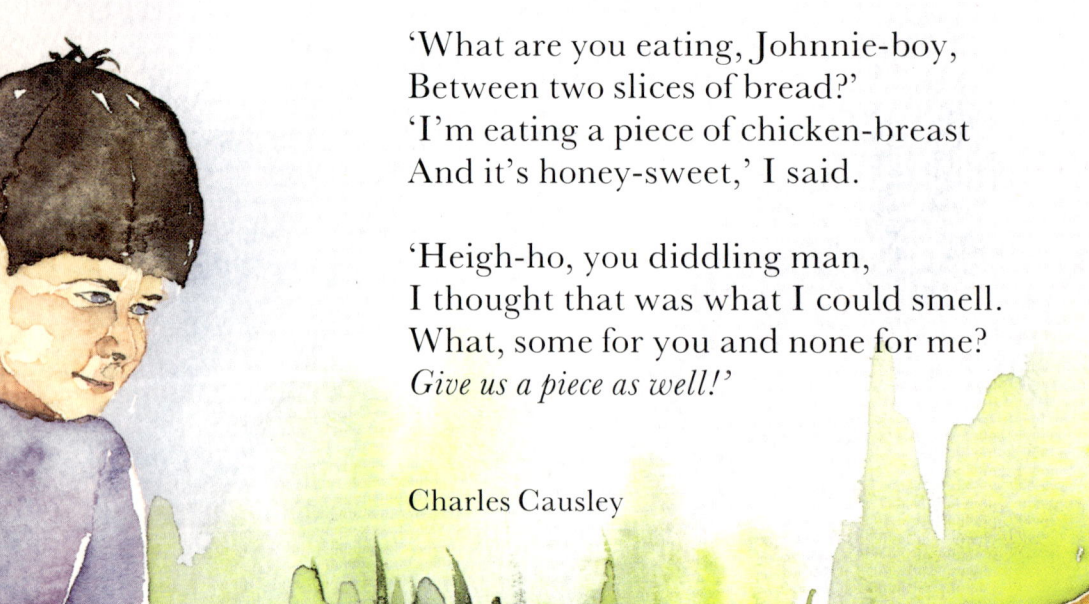

Little Trotty Wagtail

Little trotty wagtail, he went in the rain,
And tittering, tottering sideways he near got straight again,
He stooped to get a worm, and look'd up to catch a fly,
And then he flew away ere his feathers they were dry.

Little trotty wagtail, he waddled in the mud,
And left his little footmarks, trample where he would.
He waddled in the water-pudge, and waggle went his tail,
And chirrupt up his wings to dry upon the garden rail.

Little trotty wagtail, you nimble all about,
And in the dimpling water-pudge you waddle in and out;
Your home is nigh at hand, and in the warm pigsty,
So, little Master Wagtail, I'll bid you a good-bye.

John Clare

Winter

When icicles hang by the wall,
    And Dick the shepherd blows his nail,
And Tom bears logs into the hall,
    And milk comes frozen home in pail;
When blood is nipped, and ways be foul,
Then nightly sings the staring owl.
Tu-whit, to-who! a merry note,
While greasy Joan doth keel the pot.

When all aloud the wind doth blow,
    And coughing drowns the parson's saw,
And birds sit brooding in the snow,
    And Marian's nose looks red and raw,
When roasted crabs hiss in the bowl,
Then nightly sings the staring owl,
Tu-whit, tu-who! a merry note,
While greasy Joan doth keel the pot.

William Shakespeare
from Love's Labour's Lost

The Sniffle

In spite of her sniffle,
Isabel's chiffle.
Some girls with a sniffle
Would be weepy and tiffle;
They would look awful,
Like a rained-on waffle,
But Isabel's chiffle
In spite of her sniffle.
Her nose is more red
With a cold in her head,
But then, to be sure,
Her eyes are bluer.
Some girls with a snuffle,
Their tempers are uffle,
But when Isabel's snivelly
She's snivelly civilly,
And when she is snuffly
She's perfectly luffly.

Ogden Nash

Snow in the Suburbs

    Every branch big with it,
      Bent every twig with it;
  Every fork like a white web-foot;
  Every street and pavement mute:
Some flakes have lost their way, and grope back upward, when
Meeting those meandering down they turn and descend again.
  The palings are glued together like a wall,
  And there is no waft of wind with the fleecy fall.

    A sparrow enters a tree,
      Whereon immediately
  A snow-lump thrice his own slight size
  Descends on him and showers his head and eyes,
      And overturns him,
      And near inurns him,
  And lights on a nether twig, when its brush
Starts off a volley of other lodging lumps with a rush.

    The steps are a blanched slope,
      Up which, with feeble hope,
  A black cat comes, wide eyed and thin;
      And we take him in.

Thomas Hardy

Sparrow

He's no artist.
His taste in clothes is more
dowdy than gaudy.
And his nest – that blackbird, writing
pretty scrolls on the air with the gold nib of his beak,
would call it a slum.

To stalk solitary on lawns,
to sing solitary in midnight trees,
to glide solitary over gray Atlantics –
not for him: he'd rather
a punch-up in a gutter.

He carries what learning he has
lightly – it is, in fact, based only
on the usefulness whose result
is survival. A proletarian bird.
No scholar.

But when winter soft-shoes in
and these other birds –
ballet dancers, musicians, architects –
die in the snow
and freeze to branches,
watch him happily flying
on the O-levels and A-levels
of the air.

Norman MacCaig

Winter Poem

Deep and crisp and even
The snow lay roundabout,
As we went walking
Through a Bohemian winter
On the untrodden ground.

The sun struck blue and silver
From the whiteness we walked
Till snow fell, and then
Through spires of trees
Angels and giants stalked.

Gerda Mayer

Santa Claus

I won't go to sleep

Fur coat, fur hat, and fur-lined gloves,
And now he pulls his snowboots on.
His sledge is piled with sacks and sacks:
I'll wish again before it's gone.

I won't go to sleep

He walks the paddock deep in snow,
He harnesses his reindeer team.
The reindeer snort and shake their heads;
Their bells and harness-buckles gleam.

I WON'T go to sleep

Their comet rises through the air;
Fast-falling snowflakes pass them by.
With silent hooves and shaken bells
They stream across the starlit sky.

I . . . won't . . . go . . . to . . .

Clive Sansom

What the Donkey Saw

No room in the inn, of course,
And not that much in the stable,
What with the shepherds, Magi, Mary,
Joseph, the heavenly host —
Not to mention the baby
Using our manger as a cot.
You couldn't have squeezed another cherub in
For love or money.

Still, in spite of the overcrowding,
I did my best to make them feel wanted.
I could see the baby and I
Would be going places together.

U. A. Fanthorpe

A Peculiar Christmas

Snow? Absolutely not.
In fact, the weather's quite hot.
At night you can watch this new
Star without catching the 'flu.

Presents? Well, only three.
But then there happen to be
Only three guests. No bells,
No robins, no fir-trees, no smells

– I mean of roast turkey and such:
There are whiffs in the air (a bit much!)
Of beer from the near public house,
And of dirty old shepherds, and cows.

The family party's rather
Small – baby, mother and father –
Uncles, aunts, cousins dispersed.
Well, this Christmas *is* only the first.

                                    Roy Fuller

Halfway Down

Halfway down the stairs
Is a stair
Where I sit.
There isn't any
Other stair
Quite like
It.
I'm not at the bottom,
I'm not at the top;
So this is the stair
Where
I always
Stop.

Halfway up the stairs
Isn't up,
And isn't down.
It isn't in the nursery,
It isn't in the town.
And all sorts of funny thoughts
Run round my head:
'It isn't really
Anywhere!
It's somewhere else
Instead!'

A.A. Milne

The Black Cloud

Little flocks of peaceful clouds,
    Lying in your fields so blue,
While my eyes look up they see
    A black Ram coming close to you.

He will scatter you poor flocks,
    He will tear up north and south;
Lightning will come from his eye,
    And fierce thunder from his mouth.

Little flocks of peaceful clouds,
    Soon there'll be a dreadful rout,
That Ram's horns can toss big ships,
    Tear an oak tree's bowels out.

W.H. Davies

Snowball Wind

The wind was throwing snowballs.
It plucked them from the trees
and tossed them all around the woods
as boldly as you please.

I ducked beneath the spruces
which didn't help a speck;
the wind kept throwing snowballs
and threw one down my neck.

Aileen Fisher

Dust of Snow

The way a crow
Shook down on me
The dust of snow
From a hemlock tree

Has given my heart
A change of mood
And saved some part
Of a day I had rued.

Robert Frost

In December

Cattle are crowding the salt-lick.
The gruel of mud icily thickens.
On the farm-boy's Honda a sweat of fog drops.
They are logging the woodland, the sole standing crop.

Charles Tomlinson

Questioning Faces

The winter owl banked just in time to pass
And save herself from breaking window glass.
And her wings straining suddenly aspread
Caught color from the last of evening red
In a display of underdown and quill
To glassed-in children at the windowsill.

Robert Frost

Small, Smaller

I thought that I knew all there was to know
Of being small, until I saw once, black against the snow,
A shrew, trapped in my footprint, jump and fall
And jump again and fall, the hole too deep, the walls too tall.

Russell Hoban

End of a Cold Night

The pond has closed its frozen eyelid,
The grass clump clenched its frozen claws.
The sky wheels like a millstone dropping grains
Of frost through air drawn thin and clear as glass.

The moon lies bleaching on the hedges.
A cock crows thinly and far away
– And a spell is broken; suddenly Time scratches
The hour on its box and up flares a new day.

Norman MacCaig

The Old Wife and the Ghost

There was an old wife and she lived all alone
   In a cottage not far from Hitchin:
And one bright night, by the full moon light,
   Comes a ghost right into her kitchen.

About that kitchen neat and clean
   The ghost goes pottering round.
But the poor old wife is deaf as a boot
   And so hears never a sound.

The ghost blows up the kitchen fire,
   As bold as bold can be;
He helps himself from the larder shelf,
   But never a sound hears she.

He blows on his hands to make them warm,
   And whistles aloud 'Whee-hee!'
But still as a sack the old soul lies
   And never a sound hears she.

From corner to corner he runs about,
   And into the cupboard he peeps;
He rattles the door and bumps on the floor,
   But still the old wife sleeps.

Jangle and bang go the pots and pans,
   As he throws them all around;
And the plates and mugs and dishes and jugs,
   He flings them all to the ground.

Madly the ghost tears up and down
   And screams like a storm at sea;
And at last the old wife stirs in her bed –
   And it's 'Drat those mice,' says she.

Then the first cock crows and morning shows
   And the troublesome ghost's away.
But oh! what a pickle the poor wife sees
   When she gets up next day.

'Them's tidy big mice,' the old wife thinks,
   And off she goes to Hitchin,
And a tidy big cat she fetches back
   To keep the mice from her kitchen.

James Reeves

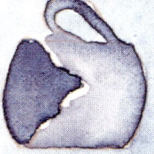

At Middle-Field Gate in February

The bars are thick with drops that show
    As they gather themselves from the fog
Like silver buttons ranged in a row,
And as evenly spaced as if measured, although
    They fall at the feeblest jog.

They load the leafless hedge hard by,
    And the blades of last year's grass.
While the fallow ploughland turned up nigh
In raw rolls, clammy and clogging lie –
    Too clogging for feet to pass.

How dry it was on a far-back day
    When straws hung the hedge and around,
When amid the sheaves in amorous play
In curtained bonnets and light array
    Bloomed a bevy now underground!

Thomas Hardy

A Patch of Old Snow

There's a patch of old snow in a corner
    That I should have guessed
Was a blow-away paper the rain
    Had brought to rest.

It is speckled with grime as if
    Small print overspread it,
The news of a day I've forgotten –
    If I ever read it.

Robert Frost

Death of a Snowman

I was awake all night,
Big as a polar bear,
Strong and firm and white.
The tall black hat I wear
Was draped with ermine fur.
I felt so fit and well
Till the world began to stir
And the morning sun swell.
I was tired, began to yawn;
At noon in the humming sun
I caught a severe warm;
My nose began to run.
My hat grew black and fell,
Was followed by my grey head.
There was no funeral bell,
But by tea-time I was dead.

Vernon Scannell

Last Snow

Although the snow still lingers
Heaped on the ivy's blunt webbed fingers
And painting tree-trunks on one side,
Here in this sunlit ride
The fresh unchristened things appear,
Leaf, spathe and stem,
With crumbs of earth clinging to them
To show the way they came
But no flower yet to tell their name,
And one green spear
Stabbing a dead leaf from below
Kills winter at a blow.

Andrew Young

Acknowledgements

Culford Books wish to thank the following for their kind permission to use their material:

'A Fox Came Into My Garden' Charles Causley from COLLECTED POEMS Macmillian. 'The Black Cloud' W.H. Davies from THE COMPLETE POEMS OF W.H. DAVIES Faber & Faber by permission of the Executors of the W.H. Davies Estate. 'The Horseman' Walter de la Mare by permission of The Literary Trustees of Walter de la Mare and The Society of Authors as their representative. 'Prelude I' T.S. Eliot from COLLECTED POEMS 1909-1962 BY T.S. ELIOT Faber & Faber. 'What the Donkey Saw' U.A. Fanthorpe from POEMS FOR CHRISTMAS Harry Chambers/Peterloo Poets. 'Snowball Wind' Aileen Fisher from IN THE WOODS, IN THE MEADOW, IN THE SKY Charles Scribner's Sons by permission of the author. 'Questioning Faces', 'Dust of Snow' and 'Patch of Old Snow' Robert Frost from THE POETRY OF ROBERT FROST edited by Edward Connery Lathem Jonathan Cape by permission of the Estate of Robert Frost and Henry Holt & Co Inc. 'A Peculiar Christmas' Roy Fuller from UPRIGHT DOWNFALL poems by Barbara Giles, Roy Fuller and Adrian Rumble (1983) Oxford University Press. 'Small, Smaller' Russell Hoban from ALL SORTS OF POEMS edited by Ann Thwaite Angus & Robertson (UK). 'Sparrow', 'End of a Cold Night', Norman MacCaig from COLLECTED POEMS BY NORMAN MACCAIG Chatto & Windus. 'Winter' Gerda Mayer by permission of the author. 'Halfway Down' A.A. Milne from WHEN WE WERE VERY YOUNG Methuen Children's Books & McClelland & Steward, Toronto. 'The Sniffle' Ogden Nash from I WOULDN'T HAVE MISSED IT 1983 Andre Deutsch. 'The Old Wife and the Ghost' James Reeves © James Reeves Estate. Reprinted by permission of The James Reeves Estate. 'Santa Claus' Clive Sansom from THE GOLDEN UNICORN Metheun. 'Fox' Laurence Smith from CATCH THE LIGHT: poems by Laurence Smith, Gregory Harrison, and Vernon Scannell (1982) Oxford University Press. 'Death of a Snowman' © Vernon Scannell. 'In December' Charles Tomlinson from COLLECTED POEMS (1985) Oxford University Press. 'Last Snow' Andrew Young from THE POETICAL WORKS OF ANDREW YOUNG Martin Secker & Warburg.

A MACDONALD BOOK

This collection of poetry © Jennifer Wilson 1987
Introduction © Jennifer Wilson 1987
Illustration © Graham Cooper 1987
FOUR SEASONS POETRY BOOKS © Culford Books 1987

First published in Great Britain in 1987 by
Macdonald & Company (Publishers) Ltd London & Sydney
A BPCC plc company
All rights reserved

Conceived, edited, designed and produced by Culford Books,
Sunningwell House, Sunningwell, Abingdon,
Oxfordshire OX13 6RD
House Editor Penelope Miller
Designed by Judith Allan
Photoset by Forruna Ltd

Printed and bound in Great Britain by
Purnell Book Production Ltd

Macdonald & Company (Publishers) Ltd,
Greater London House, Hampstead Road,
London NW1 7QX

British Library Cataloguing in Publication Data
Winter. —— (Four seasons poetry).
  1. Winter —— Juvenile poetry 2. Children's poetry, English
  I. Wilson, Jennifer II. Cooper, Graham
  III. Series
  821'.008'033   PZ8.3

ISBN 0-356-13273-0